OTHER BOOKS BY JEFFREY CYPHERS WRIGHT

Translust
Employment of the Apes
Charges
Two (with Yvonne Jacquette)
Take Over
Over the Years, An Oral History of Harlem
All in All
Walking on Words
Drowning Light
Flourish
The Name Poems
October Centerfold (with Nathaniel Hester)

Editor with Elinor Nauen of the anthology
Three Zero/ Turning Thirty

Triple Crown

Three Crowns of Sonnets
Jeffrey Cyphers Wright

SPUYTEN DUYVIL
New York City

Acknowledgements

The author wishes to thank the cool editors of the cool publications where some of these poems have appeared: *Beet, Bicycle Review, Big Bridge, Big Hammer, The Brooklyn Rail, Evergreen Review, First Literary Review – East, Eccolinguist, eightelevenpointfiftyfour, Howling Dog, Live Mag!, Maintenant, Paper Dollz, Playspace, Plush, Polarity, Reading Dance, Stretching Panties, Tribes Magazine* and *Vanitas*.

Thanks to James and Marlene Yu and The Rainforest Art Foundation for publishing the second crown. And to Bruce Weber for including me in art exhibitions and publishing sonnets in *Waltzing in Quicksand, Poets in Collage*.

Very special thanks also to Cindy Hochman and Lori Jane Ortiz for invaluable advice, encouragement, editing and proofreading assistance.

Copyright © 2013 by Jeffrey Cyphers Wright
ISBN 978-1-881471-23-3
Cover art by René Ricard and Jeffrey Cyphers Wright
Inside art by Jeffrey Cyphers Wright

Library of Congress Cataloging-in-Publication Data

Wright, Jeffrey C. (Jeffrey Cyphers)
Triple crown sonnets / Jeffrey Cyphers Wright.
p. cm.
ISBN 978-1-881471-23-3
1. Sonnets, American. I. Title.
PS3573.R5365T75 2012
811'.54--dc22
2012025951

for Ted Berrigan

Triple Crown is a modern interpretation of a traditional form. It is composed of three crowns (fifteen sonnets each) with an introductory poem for each section. It was conceived as a long serial poem that hosts numerous internal dialogues, echoes and audiences. Nevertheless, despite being embedded in a structural arch, most lines can stand starkly alone as can the poems.

The book opens in imaginary space, Lilliput, which has nevertheless been colonized (by literature and its audience). As such, it exists in an arena of activated metatext, indeterminate but predisposed.

It is an attempt to anthropomorphize time (its "paw prints") and poetry ("running on all fours"). The seasons progress as a year's cycle transpires.

All 7 continents are included and the poems are pan-mythic.

Emily Brontë is alternately a muse, a doppelgänger, a lover, a sister and a stand-in for the reader, when I address her. Or undress her, as the case may be, as one aim of poetry is seduction.

The correlative of Emily B as a particle in entanglement theory and spooky action at a distance brings current physics into the text. By choosing a muse from the past, the concept of entanglement, of two separate particles being joined in some mysterious way, expands the phenomenon from particles to persons. It opens a channel into time as well as the constructs of the imagination that exist culturally in a suspended form, like Lilliput—or Valhalla or Olympus.

Jeffrey Cyphers Wright
2012, NYC

"Fair Phoebus, leade me to the Muses springs."
  from Marlowe's translation of Ovid's *Elegies*

"Give yourself an assignment." Molly Peacock

contents

Made in Lilliput	3
Made in China	7
Made in Hong Kong	8
Made in LA	9
Made in Harlem	10
Made in Cambria	11
Made in Cucamonga	12
Made in Ithaca	13
Made in Pamplona	14
Made in Tasmania	15
Made in Gaul	16
Made in Peru	17
Made in Lhasa	18
Made in Flint	19
Made in Wales	20
Made in Khartoum	21
Made in Thrace	23
Made in Terre Haute	27
Made in Firenze	28
Made in Cheyenne	29

Made in Tinseltown	30
Made in Olympia	31
Made in Burma	32
Made in Nome	33
Made in Naples	34
Made in Babylon	35
Made in Jungleland	36
Made in Pago Pago	37
Made in Carthage	38
Made in Jerusalem	39
Made in Mustang	40
Made in Tombstone	41
Made in Java	43
Made in Valhalla	47
Made in Gotham	48
Made in Corinth	49
Made in Jasper	50
Made in Cimarron	51
Made in Lahore	52
Made in Santa Cruz	53
Made in Lillehammer	54
Made in Antarctica	55
Made in Freeport	56
Made in Siam	57
Made in Walla Walla	58
Made in Mandalay	59
Made in Honolulu	60
Made in Providence	61

Triple Crown

made in LILLIPUT

Dear Emily, I'm writing to say this is a forgery
A freak squall blown up suddenly
Dear Emily, now we are entanglement
Dear Emily, a spooky correlation-spike
Dear Emily, oil futures up this morning
On the site of the abject joy
Where the wind designs our entropy
Where we build, Dear Em, the dam of dreams
And leave no room for Death
You alone are pre-approved moodswing bingo
Dawn's lips ever plastered to your mug
Renegade parading on la Rue de Coeur
Let us dance on all fours, Emily
Like a reckless pookah caught in the grille

CROWN
I

made in CHINA

Come on down to my boat, baby
Ready to flame the lawless airbrake
Ready to dazzle the bedraggled marmadukes
Ready to fray the nightie of Big Foot
Tell me about it, Hermes
Chupacabre to the rescue
Because we have yet to reinvent the past
Ink from the pen, the filthy sun begging
I woke, a carpenter measuring my remains
Ready to rip the bark off the stars
And claw my way in looking for grubs
A psychotropic melody strips the veneer
Scrolling down Emily Brontë's heart
Ready for anything, you can see clearly now

made in HONG KONG

Come to me now, unkind whirlwind
Come to me now and unwind, wunderkind
Is it too late to come over?
Look for me in the crosswalk smackdown
Your eyes mimicking pullover lights
Come to me now, doghouse central
Come to my innocent euphoria
Snarling hosanna in the crowded stairwells
All the prestige of a Truck Route
Come silently to the shadow dome
Savor without measure the daisies warbling
Redial the future fraught with spindrift
Enlist me in your arresting farewell
Essential as a permanent white twitch

made in LA

Narcissus has nothing on you, intolerable thing
WHILE YOU WERE OUT SUFFERING
"Don't change, just lie." Ryan Adams
WHILE YOU WERE OUT HUNTING FOR MONOTONY
REEKING WITH GRANDEUR
Don't change the channel the coroner whispered
I woke up in a chamber of screaming bliss
Emily Brontë dreamed Larry Fagin at the Zinc Bar
And you were quoting Varya in The Cherry Orchard
The bartender asked Piper for her ID
Thrill jockeys spiraling like zombie vultures
The driveway spouting lost foreclosure
A one-eyed seagull staring at a pilot light
Like a fossil injected into La Brea Tar Pits

made in HARLEM

Everything is dying to be different
Except the exceptional
Aim low and keep your good side to the camera
Between Sartoris and satori
Waiting for the light to change
Lord of the wolfcopters
"Take Me To the Riot"
A Norte to End On
Knocked off my perch
And the Karma Bus is playing Paradise Lounge
And Emily Brontë is ready for her rendition
Eyes full of clearness
Even when the line goes dead
No one will erase this trace

made in CAMBRIA

Language prevents visibility from failing
Language unpeels the immediacy
Ready to apologize for interrupting
Language speaks and having spoken
Diagrams the phony traps of grammar
Velvet moss succession, language
Greens the laws of mutual addition
Stitching the preamble into your dress
Full moon tow-heaves its white carcass
Across the vault-cracked, black sky
Language appeals to second nature
Emily Brontë, naked and baying
Why are the heartstrings all ajangle
Look, even the clerk of dust lives for love

made in CUCAMONGA*

Astarte walks through the Negro streets at dawn
I said a hey babe, you are everything you are to me
Let's throw some darts at the imagination farmers
Taketh my hand and lead me on
Exult in your originality, phantom grafter
VISIGOTHS PLAYING AT HELL'S DRIVE-IN
Astarte lies under the stars in Bernadette's dream
Camilla threw her javelin across the Tiber
I woke in the fugitive tunnel glow
Emily Brontë [mug shot] dying for sanctuary
Deserted abruptly   Time's raft   Pitch and toss
This is what they say about you, Astarte
The lion, the horse, the sphinx, the dove

*Shoshone for "sandy place"

made in ITHACA

As time trickles through the Chambre des Deputes
The tendrils of my nose crinkle at its acrid passage
Time empties out the notion of originality
Time, you are a nervous imposter
You can remake yourself in the blink of an eye
Rodin pestering Phidias, Nestor attesting to glory
Time loves the one who knows love
I guess you had better guide me through the ropes
I dream a white robe walking to Morgantown
My broken watch weeps in a false spring
I wake bound to the railroad tracks
Emily Brontë sitting beside me on a wasp nest
We wait inconsolably in our vast ardor
As time trickles through an excess of small delays

made in PAMPLONA

Stick with the problem, buster
Nor mock the humming futilism
Phaedra nowhere more afraid than here
In the open air, avec désespoir
With my oar steaming I press on
Far from the Rappahannock
Seaward bound and downhill running
Never too much love beyond forever
Pipsqueak and the Melody Harvesters
Ever since Cinderella gave you the slip
Buffeted by a clique of chic tramps
Each one a symbol of uniqueness
Lost in a barrel of empathy
Like asking for a loaded blank

made in TASMANIA

Doormat: "Bad Girls Welcome"
Hungry weather chomping my antennae
Chipped words stuffing my mouth gob
Squeezing form out of absent idols
To leave behind a trace in space
I woke in an avalanche of seconds
My heart enabling the Speedlink port
With the jumper trick flash hook
Emily deploying a critical Strike Witch
Nothing can get in our way
FOR REAL
Check out the Snow Nymph's homepage
Thunder married to the dream roar
Death we made rear up and beg

made in GAUL

You have to push yourself; it's all up to you now
That's what we came for into the north wind
On each foot a compass strapped down wiggling
Ah, Penelope, we are undone by truth's hope
"Excavating the future" we prepare for the race
How long my oars have slapped the sea's wounds
Our greatness buried in tons of tongues
We heard the Police, "Bring on the Night"
Hours spilling like ink in a cave
I cover the Chambre des Deputes with foxgloves
Now it's time to listen for the caterpillar
As May spins its wrecked gentians
Poetry as a window wiper or comet's tail
Lavender Diamond sings — "Remember our love"

made in PERU

Crash cultivate a casual countenance
Zombie amoebas overtaking Paradise Lounge
Instigate a No Holds Barred policy for guests
Long Live the Nitro Hawks and all their ilk
Emily Brontë — give me your furlined poon
I'll hound you till the ends of encroachment
No sooner said than done in with a shovel
Bury my heart where the wild things are
At the intersection of knuckle and sandwich
No longer will I fight from here to wherever
The poem as a recording from your mother
The poem as a giant Jabberwock in leotards
What Ho! Take me to your leotard, starmite
Dance with the nickled silence reapers

made in LHASA

The artist needs to whittle out a forest
Ebony, calabur, ash and jacaranda
Cross-grafted to the limb vault
I need to hang the sky from my tongue
Re-enter a new version of the past
On track and on time, but behind
The croak hinges of my throat crack
Black anthem of the veined runway
This is where they'll finally bring you
Place of the gods where Padmasambhava
(Born on a lotus pad on Lake Dhanakosha)
Pinned down the earth demoness
Kicking and screaming in a tailspin
Slow-dancing with the nickled silence

FLINT

My glockenspiel is better than your glockenspiel
Where are the morons when you need them?
His family was in the iron and steel business
His mother ironed and his father stole, Lola said
At The Half Gallery for Rene Ricard's show
Behoove!
What are the chances, alive in the ruins?
"English Idylls" by George Butterworth sounds good
Fusebound to Emily Brontë's hot pussy snatch
I woke in the briar patch, pricker beset
Hebe sowing discord among Maimonides' followers
I wouldn't have it any other way, stomach knot
The river still polishes its pewter bowl
Carrying its bluejack face around, looking up

made in WALES

Thence it was you embarked upon a lark
You put on a glass slipper, thence t'was clear
Honor-bound, you're here to see it through
Crepe myrtle whipping the air you breathe
Corporeal whelps sucking at your eyeballs
Annihilation ticking its black fever clock
Whence — whither — witheringly winsome
Phaedra has nowhere to hide so come here
Minos will judge only the dead, so live
Remain where you are — don't try anything
Relax; you're the sexiest thing around
AND HOW
Each cell hooks up to a rogue star direct
In time's furry ear plant your winter crop

made in KHARTOUM

Locked in the clock factory running out of time
The gate welded shut with a human torch
The Kooks "just don't care — do do, dit dit dit"
I wake up exiled from immediacy
My eyes burning in Emily Brontë's looking glass
Dire pleasures   Hereabouts
A thousand friends, not too many
Hellbent on making a punctilious mess
Amid a welter of bruising wink shudders
CRY LIKE A TEENAGE ROBOT
Row on, my Myrmidons, the shore is a cheap toy
A fighting chance to star in a marathon of love
Where the screech owl meets the squeaking gurney
Gryphon wings shed hieroglyphs in the wind

made in THRACE

United we progress toward a more perfect union
In vein, looking for a perfect mistake
Where clouds mince the way we whirr
O extravagant vacuum — humming compression
I was waiting for you to get going, wordskinner
Plunge tributary tracked with belief
GET SLOPPY
In the honeycombed recesses of August
I was ready to zap the unzipped slats
And you alone, flash-drenched and light stitched
Held the wasted love in your strained eyes
Stacking the brittle hours in a rented vault
Hammer dreams nailed to the flipper
In the spore cluster of possibility I await

CROWN
II

made in TERRE HAUTE

Hi, half-pint star-print — bewilderment continues
Pragmatism, patronage, privilege — all elude me
Penance comes in small packages
Like Phoenix licking the spoon of forever
So, I jumped the turnstile (figuratively)
Laughing all the way to the banquet
Chained to the soft monster
The poem as girlfriend
La Tour d'Argent Poinct ne Leurre*
Meet me in the observatory, in freedom's guise
Date with a wrecking ball
As hard as they come   TIMBER
I woke at the end of a punch line
Emily Brontë by my side, always happy to be alive

*"The Silver Tower Doth Not Deceive"

made in FIRENZE

Thump-bellied lightning straddler, I think
Tethered to the recent lateness
A place to visit outside the screech jolt
Concealed in the mirror's munching maw
What men die for and women fog harp
Apollo lugging a faded penumbra
Ready for anything, anytime, anywhere
Pallas Athena taking off her clunky armor
Leaving it all behind one second at a time
Flaking them off like pearl grist
Droop nests in your heart, sagging
Anxious to torch the language
Your scorching touch, a lifeline
Foam-bathed in the apologies for nothing

made in CHEYENNE

In a sense, innocence itself is a pure sin
The jester making a cameo on The Jetsons
And we gag voluntarily on the manifesto
Yanked from the crinkled cocoon
THE POEM a bum rap giving us the bum's rush
Bumblebees buzzing the butterfly bush
OH LOVE OF LOVES
I woke in the Green Zone dying to live
Emily Brontë in black bombazine pump-crocked
Her Bambi gloves totally banjo-proof
Seaweed on the dashboard, the needle spinning
The snow belled now, drifts stagger-riven
Jiggle-tumbling and frag-ripped at dawn
Aurora autographs the wind's willowed wand

made in TINSELTOWN

You will know it by its cross bill and wing bars
Alternating bouts of flapping with gliding
Always seems like forever before hand
Days of wine and rosy fingered fireworks
No more, Aurora, to find a free signifier
No more to the tower come, trespasser
I woke lashed to the spoke and gagging
Diddling Emily Brontë's fuckstiff titty nubs
Ruled by convention's readout (redoubt)
Unmoored by Hinge Theory at KGB's on East 4th
Cables of impulse tribute so inclined entwine
Season of the clutch hitter vs. the pinch hitter
It's always the external stomp duet inside
Naked and invisible on the road to La Mama Etc

made in OLYMPIA

Blue trucks of temporary immortality
Your eyes shammy sky's palimpsests
Guests etched into the meat locker
The Have-Nots have not been invited
Says the poet, "Language is a joke"*
Waitress of giant, starving vagrants
Thief of sighs on the upper bridge
Cigarette cherries punk-branding night
Born in the supertramp white nova
My black crown's orbit, decaying slips
Pledged to undertaking wang speed
The urban fury turbine undiminished
Ink cutouts cradle the cloud scuttle
Vulcan's nightcap volt arc webbed

*Andy Clausen

made in BURMA

Sick and wasted, purling at the gates
Every day a tidal wave washing over
Swamp-dashed in the cramp factory
Where loss gnaws on the news of never
NO IDLING
Snowbound and hounded by memory
Surrounded by repositories of absence
I dozed in the wheeze-rattled dollhouse
Bones clinkered and hurtle-blown
Emily Brontë refusing to stay down
Morpheus showing us how to be human
As Icarus claws the wind's mask
You mewl, white chalk on asphalt
It doesn't matter anymore who started it

made in NOME

Kickin' it off with The Dead Weather
"Hey, you from the heavens"
The artist needs to white out a blizzard
Dear Emily Brontë drizzled with jizz
Zeus set you up for a fall too, Paris
Moving down the catwalk like a simoom
In slow mo — able to enfranchise the masses
Cast in the role of a moral objective
Slaving away on my virtual tombstone
Outside the "vitrine of therapeutic mystery"
River of fevergrief, take me all the way
"Strange Times" from The Black Keys
Out of my gourd, I played myself por toi
For you, even the sky turns blue

made in NAPLES

Meet me at Café Anacreon, calm flicker-besieged
O bounty hunters of lockstep salvation
My eyes engulfed in infinite glue, I'll look
For you, Emily, where flags rout the wind
Where missionaries meet Venus from Eryx
Born in the squelch puddle drain, I'll seek you out
My court date, jack-rigged
FINAL BETS
Black is the color of my true love's crossbow
Venus asking for an ice pick in the Green Room
Cupid's mother, asking for a shaft
I watched her take a bow at the slam tonight
One more time, she hit on her true mark
And let fly an arrow to my still-beating heart

made in BABYLON

Meaningless love floods the space between us
UNSTOPPABLE AND UNENDING
Baffled by the dream's harness chafe, I woke
Emily Brontë, spit-sucked and ooze-spasmed
Boondoggled by the kerfuffle mongers
Overdrawn at the 9-Lives Branch
Every collar a burden of stiff-bundled moans
Failing to volunteer for settling
You kept antagonizing the flicker wrench
You were easy as jailbait
Your bones, gurgling, giddy geysers of blood
WANTON — DEAD OR ALIVE
It was the same when Phaedra dropped by
You'll find everything to your satisfaction

made in Jungleland

How can you dilly-dally while daffodils aspire?
Elysian night owls talon-lifting the cerulean tent
Pan asked me to be here stranded in Forever's corner
Mugwumps bogarting the joint. Fie, for shame!
Emma Goldman, lead us over the ramparts
Don't want to be in a revolution where I can't dance
My heart infected by doped lightning
Wild skanky panky, skip-handled and groove-tongued
Hanging in there, pointing out Emily Brontë to guests
I wake in the Café Telemachus   FINAL OFFER
Eileen Myles playing an A7 on my guitar
Carrying on about the next stop is Jungleland
This House of Cards is made of wind
These words hiss like missiles flying in your direction

made in PAGO PAGO

Drinking horsetail tea we ask for your pledge
Dreaming grandpaw's doodle-riddled invoices
From the Glitter and Doom Tour, 90.7 WFUV
All agog at the vast martini swell on Ganymede
You and your series of brilliant lost mazurkas
Unbatten your hatch and loosen your snood
Ghost of red shifts rails on the veranda again
Daedalus and Ariadne dancing in the labyrinth
One leg made of huckleberry wing surges
And all my efforts to fly are fodder for a farrago
As thermal increases forecast new diseases
Buntings and honeycreepers nest in my chest
Yet there's no place to hide from inner yearning
My motor runs off the fumes of egging hecklers

made in CARTHAGE

I wouldn't leave you Dido, sur le bucher, abandonnée
Who would keep your right to love in the tomb
Ready to quiver-jam the scrambler
Ready to die for a supply of uninveigled style
It is true, Eros and Aphrodite have been untrue
Now the sea with slithering tongues slanders you
My mind — a coiled wedge, rages
My heart — burst-streaming into buffer specks
The gods themselves shove me back to the galley
Who dare such edicts of interdiction deny?
"Goodbye" the ocean's mouth stuffed between us
Begging forgiveness in the unfounded light
Oh, Dido, defender of heaven's scabs
Dido, I would've swept your palace with my last hair!

made in JERUSALEM

I woke parched in the silicone gondola with Cyberjack
Emily Brontë in a bikini reading Konkueror protocol
Dream Bob's wife naked munching M&Ms
Oom pah pah   Oom pah pah
Black attacks from c file in the Dragon variation
Veronica going through the motions buzzwiped
She'll still bring us victory, bucktooth gopher server
Also see Fennec, Flock, Galeon, Gnuzilla, K-Meleon, etc.
Also Speedwell, oblong branch spikes of purple shimmer
A spray in your lapel to keep from accidents on the road
On the Rue de Coeur, wet blooms calm flicker-besieged
And legs spread bobble headed and easy pasted
To the lighthouse shadow's true webbed image
Meet me there now in the ripple threshold, Madfox

made in MUSTANG

A poker in one hand, a joker in the other
Jugglers and jongleurs toking up out back
Time hot-stoking the furnace of distension
I woke drafting the jail of dreams
Splash-rivered my face in hellfire
Emily Brontë's tranquil quim bubbling goo
EVERYTHING MUST GO
Home is where my horse is
As Broadside Press rejected me
Buddha's Revenge overpriced with a long waiting list
As 6x6 rejected me
And the hellions take their hellion exam
Looking to us all
Let me park by you Osiris in the handicapped space

made in TOMBSTONE

How swift d'ye roll, drift thruster
For whom the belles extol
I see you at the warp gate, Psyche
Ambushing the star parade
Synthesizing the blowup ID
Mounting the lost bandwidth
Struggling with bleak delight
FREE DELIVERY
A long staff for the long walk
A white owl on your right
One thing left in the ancient future
Seduce the immortals
Emily, I will hold you to the end
Beyond fear and before everything

made in JAVA

Walking with Xeena in alleys of infinite pitch
Searching for the white surge merger
Where desire and satisfaction flip for it
I wake in the holding pen
Emily Brontë giving me the what for
Befuddled by the fustian fuddy duddies
Outfoxed by a dubitable future
Too many not enoughs
Built with swing and window shuffling
The jawbone of an ass to back you
Phone ringing here at 5C Cafe
You'll always be welcome here, June bug
On this page of air I have herein inscribed
This is the line you've been waiting to stand in

CROWN III

made in VALHALLA

Hacking through the mist, bare-fanged
Facing down the freaky keister
Dragging surplus love around the hall
With Utopia on my shoulder, Atlas
My gestures straight from the tube
And the giddy tour guides gong amok
Thrash-marooned in the maze, swoon
All honor brought back from the black edge
And you could have stayed until dawn
The crown of Ishtar to be your hub
Until the jackals overtook the stragglers
Stay now, your horn of mead full on
Stay, see your face in the moon's helmet
Stay with me, lost in the Map Room

made in GOTHAM

Poseidon's colossal tears fall into Ulysses' beer
In the midnight hour sing "In the Midnight Hour"
David Shapiro's blood runs gold in his poems
His son found The Lost Son's orange dustcover
I've never found any attraction, Magneto said
Skitter-bolted to the black-eyed roadbed
Go little book; hook up to the star-docks
Lick the flame again, like Phoenix
Back up, jackass, make room for the nonbelievers
Olympus crowned with cotton fog
I polish its organ with everything I've got
Like an old puzzle laughing, its shoes untied
I will cover you with wings of garnet whoosh
Until everyone is home free and utterly Bozo

made in CORINTH

Nowhere to run on wobble legs of splay
Froth-slathered in the soup up to my ass
I woke in the lobby discombobulated
Emily Dickinson claiming insanity
Crumple-ducking the wine-red curtain
Dust Empire coating my throat, rasps
And Natalia Calderon engages public space
From a Mouffian agonist point of view
Not distinguishing between work and play
The Trobriands, according to Malinowski
Polaris getting brighter, image thrower
As Text Wrangler bites the margin grazers
And you alone are left holding the leash
Pluto behind us, looming, lights our way

made in
JASPER

Venus melting, rows ashore alone
Ghost pussy on the run
Never finished — always done
Saxophone slain in dim velvet time
As Aurora sips the morning dew
Full dipper dripping diamond fur
That's called "Kandi" by One EskimO
I wake in the stilt warehouse again
Carving limbs out of excessive joy
Let's meet in the buffer stream, Emily
Pawned by rain
Gathering bane in scribbled light
Stretcher-bound, you are looking fine
Hobbling into the hoarfrost forest again

made in CIMARRON

Almost got stranded there red rock Greyhound
Blue sky; snowing now in New York town
Glibsville, poets chasing tails 'round
Tied to a wreath, my toy heart shudder-towed
Instead try rebooting the hotbox root
The bridge hitched to a falling roar
Have to keep going like this, sugar tour
The sand keeps falling too and the hour glaze
Trick the wind into breathing love and say
Heat that flush and rush in fool
TRAWLING FOR FOOLS
I woke in the treehouse dreaming my son
You alone in the hollow flow light unconsumed
All that gold wick-splattering your curling hair

made in LAHORE

I call on Circe to channel the circus
Follow instructions: act like a ham
I beg the twin sisters to reinstall love
Mysteries to be my only mistresses
Crocus, scilla, coltsfoot and willow
White coral bells tolling for no one
Greet me on my tiny walk around
Lurch-walking on wracked limbs
Stop, drop and roll (another one)
Dream Tom Savage hands me a j
At Washington Square
Aching bright at the perigee arch
Time running away from us
Its paw prints filling the blood moat

made in SANTA CRUZ

Before we are destroyed, let Hutash
Prepare a rainbow bridge
A method for the madness
Our world, come tumbling down
Laughing all the way to the banquet
Chained to the soft monster
The Subjugator was here
At a loss for words, baying
Seek a keepsake, now release
SIGN HERE
Emily, a bell torn from the sun
I wake in a forest of cherry smoke
Love hammer in the dream spout
Heaven's tomahawk stuck in my hat

made in LILLEHAMMER

While you were sleeping snow filled the air
Clump-happy and dazzle-fused
White-stuffed, cross drafting over down
Flurry spirals and full out drift blowing
Slow into the Union tolls
This is Renegade Chris on pirate radio
You are pulling my leg, Loki, you old dog
I'm going to milk your goat if you don't watch it
Gunpowder light and shadows lantern-buried
Dizzy, swiveling and gyrating in futile euphoria
Gasping stranded, flabbergasted and flayed
Purple clamped to my pointless crown
Emily Brontë's gaping absence draws me out
I wake in the trench, overcome and spit-wet

made in ANTARCTICA

The flakes big now, white moths dazzlespun
Fine as Rapunzel's hair coming down
What were you doing all that time
I was hunting for you in the cinder palace
Your eyes, dancing boxcars on ice rails
My shriek prayer white-sparking the brake
Pegasus stomping, ready to come
Scapegoat Island and you are looking fine
Snow needle-whipped and sideways stiff
You, bamboozler of Beelzebub
What say you now?
Infinity suckers barking up the wrong tree
Nevertheless, Hiring Now
Six white horses pulling your last words away

made in FREEPORT

Dogwoods whimper outside Hotel du Monde
As time re-shuffles its dog-eared deck
Besieged by the storm's monocle
Beseeching sun to augur through felt sky
My face cut by rain on the bridge to eternity
Strewn among thistles, my wishes shred
Orpheus staring back at love's wreck
I tackle the poem running on all fours
In a rush, you leave jet earrings behind
With blinkered tears you're unable to shed
The token booth clerk yelling, "Pay your fare"
Emily Brontë forwards her unsheathed breath
I was going to go on forever and a month
But now I see you have saved the best for last

made in SIAM

Put my heart in a sling, send it to Singapore
My little songbird from Alcatraz
The Dow rose and the S&P fell
The Cubs are pitching a fit
Dream cops tailing me on Bowery
Eavesdropping on the angel exchange
Victor giving me wild leeks to eat
Cock-eyed and busted, the drawbridge stuck
Gatecrasher written all over your face
I woke lashed to the spoke, gagging
Emily Brontë retching up rune chunks
Nothing between us but terminal presence
The Virtual Host seamlessly maintained
Let me say it again, the way out is the way in

made in WALLA WALLA

Speak to me then, Gray Wolf
Let the moon hurl its guts across the sky
Ducks huddle-bobbing on glass river glance
No gate to stay forever shut
Unconsumed by the present I present the now
The Dusters tonite at Mongrel Hall
WANNA BE GOD'S TOY
Let's get hammered, Thor
Have the forlorn hopes ready to advance
Stand to, me bonny lads
Hold the line right steady
Dreamt no time to take off clown make-up
I woke, pinioned to the rack
Enslaved by the détournements of jouissance

made in MANDALAY

Born for the fray I piss into the abyss
Following haze-lighters over the falls
My job now to enlist stray hearts
Devoted only to springing freedom's trap
Before losing the wrinkle game
March's cold mask rain-slashed
Andromeda chained, prays for Perseus
Go little book, sing to the star-docks
The piper piping all hands on deck
Following the automatic love romp
I woke in the crosshairs writhing
Emily Brontë storm-lashed and wailing
Licking the bell's mournful firewall
Black clouds mingle with my ink

made in HONOLULU

Voracious in its veracity, the poem
Shaved off the haywired heart throng
Line stacks in the deathly page flaps
Enthralling contours, muse-planed
Cloudless victory as the meter burned
White buildup spool in cog relapse
April, a record high
My door stump knocking
I woke in the Boom Boom Room
Emily Brontë stripped for speed
Ever ready to die for immortality
Thrill-choking on ladder dust
We board the overarching trial
Sirensong whirling into my ear whorl

made in PROVIDENCE

Let us now upend what we've finished
Going apeshit in general
Aping the apes
Strutting and japing like a jackanapes
Say it again; the way out is the way in
Weaving home through fleeced air
My hat full of tricks, tips
Orpheus wailing in the pit
His lyre reeling down stars
The more you need the less you are
Let the river steal along its rail
On the route to the root
Source of sorcery and mask of bone
Take me back again into the unknown

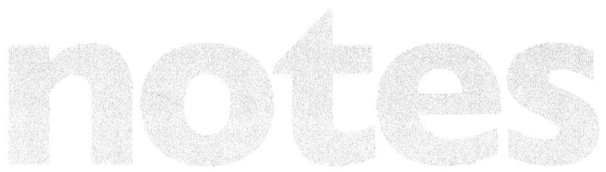

Crown I

3 MADE IN LILLIPUT

Lilliput A fictional island nation in Jonathan Swift's novel *Gulliver's Travels*, published in 1726.

Entanglement, spooky action at a distance, and correlation-spike are terms describing relationships in subatomic physics.

And leave no room for Death Emily Brontë wrote "There is not room for Death" in "No coward soul is mine." Charlotte Brontë notes of this poem, written January 2, 1846, that "The following are the last lines my sister Emily ever wrote."

Pookah A spirit as well as a modern term of endearment.

7 MADE IN CHINA

Come on down to my boat "Come On Down To My Boat," recorded by Every Mother's Son, reached number six on the Billboard charts in July of 1967.

Marmadukes The name has comical English upper-class connotations because it contains the word duke.

Tell me about it, Hermes Hermes is the herald, or messenger of the gods to humans.

You can see clearly now "I Can See Clearly Now" was written by Johnny Nash and first and recorded in 1972.

8 Made in Hong Kong

Snarling hosanna Inspired by *Hallelujah Blackout* by Alex Lemon.

Truck Route Posted on West 14th Street in New York City.

9 Made in LA

Los Angeles, California. Literally, *the angels*.

Narcissus In Greek mythology a hunter of exceptional beauty and pride. Nemesis tricked him into gazing at his reflection in a pool. Taken by his own beauty he fell in love with his image and was unable to leave.

Ryan Adams Rock star.

Larry Fagin Poet, New York School and long-time East Village resident.

Zinc Bar Originally called Club Cinderella, a jazz club where Billie Holiday appeared. Now a jazz and poetry bar.

The Cherry Orchard A 1904 play by Anton Chekov.

Thrill jockey Thrill Jockey is a record label out of Chicago. Established in 1992.

10 Made in Harlem

Harlem, New York City.

Sartoris A 1929 novel about decaying aristocracy in Mississippi by William Faulkner.

Satori A Japanese Buddhist term for enlightenment.

Wolfcopter A DJ since March 3, 2009.

"Take Me To The Riot" A song by Stars from their 2007 album *In Our Bedroom After the War*.

A Norte to End On A confabulation of the phrase "to end on a high note" and the 1983 movie *El Norte*.

Karma Bus In this context it is a fake rock and roll band but the phrase means that you will receive your just amount of karma, good or bad, based on your actions.

Rendition Legalese for handing over detainees to another country for torturous interrogations that are illegal in the United States.

11 Made in Cambria

Cambria The ancient name for Wales. Also the default typeface for Mac computers.

12 Made in Cucamonga

Cucamonga, California. Cucamonga probably means "sandy place" in the native tongue or Shoshone language.

Astarte Chief female goddess of the Eastern Mediterranean and is connected to fertility, sexuality, and war. Her symbols include **the lion, the horse, the sphinx, the dove.**

Negro streets Allen Ginsberg's "Howl": "…Negro streets at dawn…"

Bernadette Mayer, poet, told me Astarte was her favorite god.

Camilla The "warrior virgin" and a servant to Diana. As an infant, her father tied her to a javelin and threw it across a river to save her. Virgil claims she had divine power and ran so swiftly the grass turned to ash.

13 Made in Ithaca

Ithaca, New York. Ithaca, the island in the Ionian Sea, Greece. Home of Odysseus.

Chambre des deputes The name given to several parliamentary bodies in the nineteenth and twentieth centuries beginning with the Bourbon Restoration. The final assembly evolved to the point of being elected by universal suffrage, in which every one voted.

Time empties out the notion of originality Refers to notions of identity, appropriation, and originality formulatedby Roland Barthes in his 1967 essay "The Death of the Author" by Roland Barthes in his 1967 essay "The Death of the Author" and to *Simulacra and Simulation* by Jean Baudrillard.

Phidias The 5th century BC Greek sculptor was accused of stealing precious materials from commissions to make his own art. He died in prison.

Nestor An Argonaut and a man of "sweet words." In the Iliad he was already old when the war began and he talks about former glory, gives advice to younger warriors, and urges reconciliation between Agamemnon and Achilles.

14 Made in Pamplona

Pamplona, Spain is famous for the running of the bulls.

Phaedra The name derives from the Greek word for bright. She is the daughter of Minos and Pasiphaë. Her story is included in two plays by Euripides, of which one survives. Though married to Theseus, she fell in love with Hippolytus.

Far from the Rappahannock From "Into the Dusk Charged Air" by poet John Ashbery.

Pipsqueak and the Melody Harvesters A fake rock band.

15 Made in Tasmania

The Australian island, Tasmania.

Speedlink A verb meaning to round up a collection of links to other blogs' posts. It was also a wagonload freight service operated by British Rail from 1977 to 1991.

Strike Witch Anime figures from television and film.

16 MADE IN GAUL

Gaul was a region of Western Europe including all of France during the Iron Age and Roman Era.

Penelope In the Odyssey, Penelope is the faithful wife of Odysseus.

Excavating the future *City of Quartz: Excavating the Future in Los Angeles* is a 1990 book by Mike Davis. It explores the different ideas of the city from "sunny" to "noir" and ends with the "junkyard of dreams."

The Police An English rock band formed in London in 1977 and fronted by Sting.

Chambre des deputes See Made in Ithaca.

Lavender Diamond Los Angeles-based folk/country-pop quartet.

17 MADE IN PERU

Where the Wild Things Are Maurice Sendack's 1963 children's picture book.

Nitro Hawks A fake band name. Also a remote-controlled model car.

Bury my heart The book *Bury My Heart at Wounded Knee* by Dee Brown was published in 1970. It's also the title of a song released by Buffy St. Marie and the Waterboys.

Jabberwock The Jabberwock was a fictional character in Lewis Carroll's nonsense verse poem, "Jabberwocky."

Take me to your leotard A malapropism for "Take me to your leader."

18 MADE IN LHASA

Lhasa, Tibet.

Padmasambhava In Sanskrit means "Lotus-Born." He came into this world to teach the Tantras and is known as the "second Buddha." He was from Waziristan, Pakistan, the lawless tribal region bordering Afghanistan.

19 MADE IN FLINT

Flint, Michigan.

Half Gallery A pop up gallery run by Vito Schnabel.

Rene Ricard Warholian film actor, artist and poet.

George Butterworth English composer, 1885 - 1916.

Hebe Greek goddess of youth and a cupbearer on Mt. Olympus. She is the daughter of Zeus and Hera and wife of Hercules. Her sister is Eris, the Spirit of Discord.

Maimonides 1135–1204. Foremost Jewish theologian and

philosopher. He synthesized Aristotelian thought and Biblical faith. His writings stirred up great debate.

20 MADE IN WALES

Wales is a country in the United Kingdom with its own language.

Glass slipper What Cinderella wore.

Phaedra See Made in Pamplona.

Minos King of Crete and son of Zeus. His daughters include Phaedra and Ariadne. His wife Pasiphaë was cursed by Poseidon to lust after a white bull; to attract it, she hid inside a hollowed wooden cow. They bore the bull-headed child Minotaur (Minotauros, "the bull of Minos").

21 MADE IN KHARTOUM

Khartoum, Sudan.

Kooks A British rock band from Sussex.

Myrmidons Described as brave warriors commanded by Achilles in Homer's *Iliad*. They were all descendants of Myrmidon who was the son of Zeus.

Crown II

23 MADE IN THRACE

Thrace was an ancient area which was largely encompassed by present day Bulgaria. The people were a group of Indo-European tribes allied with Trojans against the Greeks in the *Iliad*. In mythology, Thrax (by his name representative of all Thracians) is a son of Ares, god of war.

United we progress toward a more perfect union Slogan for Barack Obama on a 2008 Shepard Fairey design.

The way we whirr Political activism, personal conviction, and romance don't mix in the 1973 film *The Way We Were* about Hollywood blacklisting.

27 MADE IN TERRE HAUTE

Terre Haute, Indiana. Means high ground.

Phoenix A mythological bird that symbolizes immortality. The beautiful bird lives 500 to 1000 years. After building a nest, bird and nest ignite and from the ashes the bird comes back, although some stories portray the new Phoenix as an offspring of the older one.

La Tour d'Argent Poinct ne Leurre Motto of a Parisian restaurant open since the 16th century.

Hard as they come *The Harder They Come* / the harder they fall. Jamaican crime film and title song from 1972 starring reggae singer Jimmy Cliff.

28 Made in Firenze

Firenze is how Italians refer to Florence, Italy.

Apollo Sun god whose antithesis would be a shadow, or "penumbra."

Pallas Athena Greek goddess of wisdom, courage, inspiration, arts, skill.

29 Made in Cheyenne

Cheyenne, Wyoming

The Jetsons Animated sitcom about a futuristic family. Originally on TV in 1962-63.

Green Zone A protected area in Baghdad, Iraq during the Second Gulf War.

Bambi 1942 Disney film about a young deer growing up in the woods after his mother is shot by hunters.

Aurora Goddess of dawn.

30 MADE IN TINSELTOWN

Tinseltown is a nickname for Hollywood.

You will know it by... A type of bird known as a wing-barred crossbill.

Days of wine and rosy A conflation of "Days of wine and roses" from Ernest Dowson's 1896 poem "Vitae Suma Brevis" (made into a film in 1962) and Homer's epithet "rosy fingered dawn."

No more to the tower come "Childe Roland to the Dark Tower Came" is a poem by Lord Byron.

Hinge Theory A poetic practice developed by James Heller Levinson. An essay by Allan Parsons which quotes Roger LaPorte and Jacques Derrida.

KGB's Legendary literary bar, theater and reading spot on East 4th Street in New York's East Village.

La MaMa ETC Legendary performance organization also on East 4th Street.

31 MADE IN OLYMPIA

Olympia, Washington. Olympia, Greece was the site of a sanctuary and was reputed to have been home of the Olympics in classical times.

Black crown's orbit, decaying Orbital decay occurs because of atmospheric drag.

Andy Clausen American poet and friend of Allen Ginsberg, Janine Pommy Vega, and other Beats.

Vulcan Refers to the Roman god of fire (including volcanoes). He was a blacksmith.

32 MADE IN BURMA

Burma is the old name of Myanmar.

Morpheus In Greek mythology, the god of dreams. He has the ability to take any human form and appear in dreams.

Icarus Son of Daedalus with whom he was imprisoned by King Minos of Crete. When he escaped on wings of wax and feathers, he flew too close to the sun and fell from the sky.

White chalk on asphalt The bodies of accident or crime victims are circled with chalk by investigative authorities.

33 MADE IN NOME

Nome, Alaska. From the Greek for district, nomes were administrative sections of ancient Egypt.

Dead Weather An American rock band, formed in Nashville in 2009 and including Jack White.

Zeus King of the gods in Greek mythology.

Paris His mother Hecuba dreamed of a flaming torch right before Paris was born. It ostensibly foretold the downfall of Troy. Later, Zeus (in an effort to stay out of trouble himself) asked Paris to judge which of the goddesses to be the most beautiful.

Vitrine of therapeutic mystery "...Art, outside the institutional vitrine of therapeutic mystery, is never not advertising." From *The Invisible Dragon: Essays on Beauty* by Dave Hickey.

Black Keys An American rock duo formed in Akron, Ohio in 2001.

Por toi French — for you.

34 MADE IN NAPLES

Naples, Italy.

Anacreon Greek lyric poet known for drinking songs and hymns, often with amatory lyrics.

Venus Second planet from the sun. Roman goddess of love and mother of the Roman people. Cupid's mother.

Eryx A short range portable SACLOS-based wire-guided anti-tank missile. Also an ancient city and a mountain in the west of Sicily.

Black is the color of my true love's crossbow Based on "Shampoo" lyrics by Elvis Perkins.

Green Room Show business term for the place where performers wait to go on stage.

Cupid In Roman mythology, the god of desire, affection, and erotic love. In Latin his name means "desire."

35 Made in Babylon

Babylon is the ancient name for Iraq.

Phaedra See Made in Pamplona.

36 Made in Jungleland

Jungleland is a song by Bruce Springsteen on the 1975 album *Born to Run*.

Elysian Elysian Fields represent a conception of the afterlife.

Pan Greek god of the wild and of rustic music. He has small horns like a goat's and legs like those of a faun or satyr. He was also considered by the ancient Greeks to be the god of theatrical criticism.

Mugwumps Republicans who left the party to support democratic candidate Grover Cleveland in 1884. They rebelled against the financial corruption attributed to the Republican candidate.

Bogart Slang for not sharing, especially a joint. Name derived from Humphrey Bogart's habit of dangling a cigarette in the corner of his mouth indefinitely.

Fie, for shame Facetious exclamation of distaste or mock dismay. Obsolete.

Emma Goldman 1869 – 1940. Anarchist known for political activism.

Don't want to be in a revolution where I can't dance Emma Goldman's famous dictum is "A revolution without dancing is not a revolution worth having."

Telemachus Son of Odysseus and Penelope. Athene favored and helped him. Nestor royally entertained him during a journey.

Eileen Myles New York poet and author of the semi-biographical novel *Inferno*. Long time resident of the East Village.

37 MADE IN PAGO PAGO

Pago Pago, American Samoa.

Horsetail tea A cleansing diuretic, reputed to strengthen bones.

WFUV The radio station of Fordham University.

Glitter and Doom Tour A 2008 concert tour by American rock musician Tom Waits.

Ganymede In Greek mythology, Ganymede was a beautiful boy who was abducted by Zeus disguised as an eagle. He took over Hebe's job as cupbearer. His ascent is seen as representing human aspirations to become divine. Ganymede is one of Jupiter's moons, the largest in our solar system. Ganymede is also the legendary site of the signing of the Magna Carta in 1215 which first gave citizens rights under a monarchy.

Mazurka A Polish dance resembling the polka, frequently adopted as a ballet form. Also, the music accompanying the dance. Chopin wrote 69 mazurkas.

Loosen your snood From "The Code of the West" in *The Sonnets* by Ted Berrigan, 1934-1983.

Red shifts A reference to "Red Shift" by Ted Berrigan. Also, in astrophysics, redshift happens when light observed coming from an object that is moving away is proportionally increased in wavelength. It's a shift in the frequency of a photon toward lower energy, or longer wavelength.

Daedalus Means "cunning worker." He created a large dancing area for Ariadne. Also known as architect of the Labyrinth. Icarus's father.

Ariadne Daughter of King Minos of Crete. In charge of the labyrinth. Bride of Dionysus.

Thermal increases Global warming.

38 MADE IN CARTHAGE

Carthage Ancient Carthage was founded in 814 BC near Tunis, the present day capital of Tunisia.

Dido Credited with being the founder and first queen of Carthage. In Virgil's *Aeneid* she falls in love with Aeneas (supposedly at the will of Aprhodite and with the aid of an arrow from Eros). He deserts her at the orders of Mercury. The affair is managed by Juno and Venus acting in concert. Also a top-selling English singer-songwriter born in 1971.

Dido, sur le bucher, abandonee *The death of Dido*, aka *Didon abandonee* is a painting by Andrea Sacchi, 1599-1661. Literally: Dido, head on the butcher block, abandoned.

Eros Greek god of love.

Aphrodite Greek goddess of love and beauty.

39 MADE IN JERUSALEM

Jerusalem, Israel/ Palestine.

Cyberjack Name for a web browser application created in 1995.

Konkueror protocol Konkueror was developed as an autonomous web browser project using KHTML as its layout engine.

Black attacks from the c file *New York Times* chess coverage.

Veronica A female given name, a search engine, and Saint Veronica, the Jerusalem woman, who gave Jesus her veil to wipe his sweat. When he handed it back, it miraculously bore his image. The name means "bearer of victory." Folklore has its origin as a wedding of Latin and Greek terms meaning "true image."

Bucktooth gopher server Bucktooth is a modern server for the Internet Gopher gateway. Gopher protocol is an application designed for distributing, searching and retrieving documents online.

Fennec, Flock, Galeon, Gnuzilla, K-Meleon Specialized open-source software projects related to the Firefox web browser. A fennec is a small nocturnal fox found in the Sahara.

Speedwell A common name for the flowering plant Veronica.

Rue de Couer Road of the Heart.

To the lighthouse *To the Lighthouse* is a 1927 novel by Virginia Woolf.

Madfox MadFox develops software that works with Microsoft's dynamic programming language Visual Foxpro. Also an English pop rock band.

40 MADE IN MUSTANG

Mustang, Nepal.

Jongleur A traveling minstrel, poet, or entertainer in medieval England and France.

Broadside Press Created in 1965.

6x6 Magazine Published by Ugly Duckling Presse.

Osiris Egyptian god of the afterlife and father (with his sister) of Isis of Horus.

41 MADE IN TOMBSTONE

Tombstone, Arizona.

Psyche A beautiful girl loved by Eros (Cupid) who became the personification of the soul.

White owl A symbol of wisdom and an omen of death.

Crown III

43 MADE IN JAVA

Java, Indonesia. Programming language. Slang for coffee.

Xeena A text editor for Windows, Macintosh, Linux, or UNIX.

Holding pen An enclosure for cattle and by extension humans, as in demonstrations or a "holding cell" at a police station.

Swing and window shuffling Swing and shuffle are varieties of eighth note rhythms in musical composition. Window shuffling is a technique using Microsoft Windows.

Jawbone of an ass Samson smites his enemies with the jawbone of an ass in Judges 15:15.

5C Café Music and art café at 5th Street and Avenue C in New York City.

47 MADE IN VALHALLA

Valhalla, New York. Hall of the slain in Norse mythology. Located in Asgard and ruled over by Odin.

Keister Slang for buttocks.

Utopia The term was coined by Sir Thomas Moore in 1516 for his book describing a fictional island that had an ideal society.

Atlas A primordial Titan who held up the earth on his shoulder, in Greek mythology

Ishtar Assyrian and Babylonian goddess of fertility, war, love and sex. Comparable to Astarte

Horn of mead Vikings drank a honey wine called mead from horns.

48 MADE IN GOTHAM

Gotham is a fictional city best known as the home of Batman in DC Comics. Often used as a nickname for New York City.

Poseidon Greek god of the sea.

Ulysses Derived from Ulixes, the Latin name for Odysseus. Ulysses was the king of Ithaca and the hero of *The Odyssey*.

"In The Midnight Hour" A song performed originally by Wilson Pickett in 1965. Written by Guy Sebastian.

David Shapiro American poet, literary critic and art historian.

The Lost Son A 1999 novel by Eric Leclere.

Magneto The central villain in the X-Men series from

Marvel Comics.

Go little book From Lord Byron's *Don Juan*.

Phoenix See Made in Terre Haute.

Olympus The highest mountain in Greece and regarded as the abode of the twelve Olympian gods.

Bozo Quintessential clown character in the United States first appearing on television in 1949.

49 Made in Corinth

Corinth, Greece. Halfway between Athens and Sparta. Also a town in Mississippi. Of uncertain derivation, but means "satiated."

Wine-red Reference to Homer's "the wine dark sea."

Natalia Calderon engages public space / from a Mouffian agonist point of view From MaHKUzine, a publication of Utrecht School of the Arts. Natalia Calderon is a singer. ChantalMouffe is known for post-marxist political inquiry and identity theory.

Agonist is the opposite of antagonist.

Trobriands Inhabitants of the Trobriand islands off New Guinea.

Malinowski Bronislaw Malinowski was an important 20th century anthropologist.

Polaris North star.

Text Wrangler TextWrangler is a text editor for web authoring.

Pluto Ruler of Hades Venerated as an overseer of the afterlife.

50 MADE IN JASPER

Jasper, Alberta. The name is derived from Old French and means "speckled stone."

Venus Roman goddess of love, beauty, sex, prosperity and victory.

Aurora See Made in Cheyenne.

"Kandi" Song by the English band One EskimO, formed in 2005.

Buffer stream Preloading data into a reserved area (the buffer) of memory for streaming audio or visual from the internet.

51 MADE IN CIMARRON

Cimarron, New Mexico. Derived from Spanish for fugitive or runaway, akin to maroon. Wild and unruly.

Rush in fool Alexander Pope wrote "For fools rush in where angels fear to tread."

52 MADE IN LAHORE

Lahore, Pakistan. "City of lava."

Circe Goddess of magic who tried to keep Odysseus and his crew on her island. Known for transforming her enemies into animals.

White coral bells A traditional song about the flower

Tolling for no one "Toll on, thou passing bell. Ring out my doleful knell." By Acton Bell, one of the three Bell pseudonyms the Brontë sisters adopted for publication.

Roll (another one...) An allusion to the lyrics of "Don't Bogart that Joint," by Country Joe and the Fish.

Tom Savage Poet and long-time resident of New York's East Village.

53 Made in Santa Cruz

Santa Cruz, California.

Hutash Goddess of the Chumash people of Santa Cruz island. She made a rainbow bridge for them to come to the mainland and escape overcrowding.

Come tumbling down From "In the Midnight Hour." See Made in Gotham.

54 Made in Lillehammer

Lillehammer, Norway. Means "little rocky hill."

Union tolls Parkway tolls in Union, New Jersey.

Loki Norse god or jötun (which is sometimes glossed as giant). He variously tricks or helps the other gods.

55 Made in Antartica

Rapunzel A young woman with long hair who is imprisoned in a tower. From a German fairy tale included in the 1812 Grimm Brothers publication.

Pegasus Divine winged horse.

Beelzebub Another name for Satan. One of the seven princes of Hell. The name means "Lord of Flies" in Arabic.

56 Made in Freeport

Many places have settlements named Freeport, including the Bahamas, Haiti, Canada, and Freeport of Monrovia in Liberia.

Hotel du Monde Hotel of the World (fictional).

Orpheus Legendary Greek musician, poet and oracle. Called the "father of song" by Pindar, he charmed all who heard him, even stones.

57 Made in Siam

Siam is an exonym. Used as the name of Thailand before 1939.

Singapore Sling An alcoholic drink.

Songbird of Alcatraz The "Birdman of Alcatraz" was Robert Stroud, a federal prisoner who kept birds while incarcerated. The 1962 film is a fictionalized account.

Cubs Chicago baseball team.

Victor Victor Weiss is a musician, community gardener, and naturalist in New York's East Village.

58 MADE IN WALLA WALLA

Walla Walla, Washington. A Native American tribe whose name is translated as "many waters."

Thor Norse god of thunder and lightning. Viewed as the protector of mankind; he wielded Mjölnir, a powerful hammer.

Stand to, me bonny lads From the "Devonshire Carol" lyrics in the play "Warhorse."

Détournement A term borrowed from the French and associated with Situationist International publications. It means to create a vatiation on a previous work by mixing and matching.

Jouissance French. Denotes pleasure or enjoyment although in the psychoanalysis of Jacques Lacan, the term implies a surfeit of pleasure, which would result in suffering.

59 MADE IN MANDALAY

Mandalay, Myanmar. The last royal capital of Burma.

Andromeda She was chained naked to a rock by her father as a sacrifice to a sea god.

Perseus Son of Zeus and Danae who slew Medusa. He fell in love with Andromeda and rescued her.

60 MADE IN HONOLULU

Honolulu, Hawaii. Honolulu means "place of shelter."

Boom Boom Room A trendy rooftop bar in New York City.

61 MADE IN PROVIDENCE

Providence, Rhode Island. Divine guidance or care.

Jackanapes From the *Dictionary of Archaic and Provincial Words*, "jack-an-apes ... jape-worthy... to strut." Jape means joke, jest, gibe.

Orpheus See Made in Antarctica.

about

Best known as a poet, Jeff Wright is a presence. He wears many hats, figuratively (and literally)—publisher, editor, impresario, artist, musician, critic, curator and eco-activist in the community gardens of his beloved East Village. Richard Hell once introduced him as the "Mayor of the East Village."

On arriving in New York Wright studied with Ted Berrigan and Alice Notley at St. Mark's Church and served on the Poetry Project's Board. He started Hard Press, publishing over a hundred poetry postcards and books. While finishing his Masters in poetry he studied with Allen Ginsberg who wrote a forward for his fifth book, *Take Over.*

From 1986 til 2001 Wright ran a monthly: *Cover Magazine, The Underground National.* Poems, essays and interviews have appeared in numerous anthologies, catalogues and scholarly publications. He was a featured reader twice at the Museum of Modern Art's poetry series coordinated by Lita Hornick. In 2007 Wright founded a new journal of art and poetry called *Live Mag!* His own artwork has been in shows at Tribes Gallery, Turtle Point Press, AC Institute, Thomas Jaeckel Gallery among others.

Currently Wright contributes art criticism regularly to *ArtNexus* and has a column in *The Brooklyn Rail.* This is his 13th book.

On publishing Wright's poem "Touch Base" in the *Exquisite Corpse*, Andrei Codrescu called it a *"Tour de Force."* Likewise, *Triple Crown.*

List of Images

"Coffee Goth," Rene Ricard and JCW

"Scarf," JCW

"Buffalo Dancer," JCW

"Portrait of James Romberger," JCW

"Windsor," JCW

Colophon

Fonts include Berkeley Oldstyle,
Gill Sans and Hoefler Text.

SPUYTEN DUYVIL
Meeting Eyes Bindery
Triton
Lithic Scatter

8TH AVENUE   Stefan Brecht
A DAY AND A NIGHT AT THE BATHS   Michael Rumaker
ACTS OF LEVITATION   Laynie Browne
ALIEN MATTER   Regina Derieva
ANARCHY   Mark Scroggins
APO/CALYPSO   Gordon Osing
APPLES OF THE EARTH   Dina Elenbogen
APPROXIMATING DIAPASON   hastain & thilleman
ARC: CLEAVAGE OF GHOSTS   Noam Mor
THE ARSENIC LOBSTER   Peter Grandbois
ASHES RAIN DOWN   William Luvaas
AUNTIE VARVARA'S CLIENTS   Stelian Tanase
BALKAN ROULETTE   Drazan Gunjaca
THE BANKS OF HUNGER AND HARDSHIP   J. Hunter Patterson
LA BELLE DAME   Gordon Osing & Tom Carlson
BIRD ON THE WING   Juana Culhane
BLACK LACE   Barbara Henning
BLACK MOUNTAIN DAYS   Michael Rumaker
BLUEPRINTS FOR A GENOCIDE   Rob Cook
BOTH SIDES OF THE NIGER   Andrew Kaufman
BREATHING FREE   (ed.) Vyt Bakaitis
BURIAL SHIP   Nikki Stiller
BUTTERFLIES   Brane Mozetic
BY THE TIME YOU FINISH THIS BOOK
         YOU MIGHT BE DEAD   Aaron Zimmerman
CADENCES   j/j hastain
CAPTIVITY NARRATIVES   Richard Blevins
CELESTIAL MONSTER   Juana Culhane
CEPHALONICAL SKETCHES   t thilleman
CLEOPATRA HAUNTS THE HUDSON   Sarah White
CLOUD FIRE   Katherine Hastings

COLUMNS: TRACK 2   Norman Finkelstein
COLLECTED POEMS OF LEV LOSEFF   (ed.) Henry Pickford
CONSCIOUSNESS SUITE   David Landrey
THE CONVICTION & SUBSEQUENT
            LIFE OF SAVIOR NECK   Christian TeBordo
CONVICTION'S NET OF BRANCHES   Michael Heller
THE CORYBANTES   Tod Thilleman
CROSSING BORDERS   Kowit & Silverberg
DAY BOOK OF A VIRTUAL POET   Robert Creeley
DAYLIGHT TO DIRTY WORK   Tod Thilleman
THE DESIRE NOTEBOOKS   John High
DETECTIVE SENTENCES   Barbara Henning
DIARY OF A CLONE   Saviana Stanescu
DIFFIDENCE   Jean Harris
DONNA CAMERON   Donna Cameron
DON'T KILL ANYONE, I LOVE YOU   Gojmir Polajnar
DRAY-KHMARA AS A POET   Oxana Asher
EGGHEAD TO UNDERHOOF   Tod Thilleman
EROTICIZING THE NATION   Leverett T. Smith, Jr.
THE EVIL QUEEN   Benjamin Perez
EXILED FROM THE WOMB   Adrian Sangeorzan
EXTREME POSITIONS   Stephen Bett
THE FARCE   Carmen Firan
FISSION AMONG THE FANATICS   Tom Bradley
THE FLAME CHARTS   Paul Oppenheimer
FLYING IN WATER   Barbara Tomash
FORM   Martin Nakell
GESTURE THROUGH TIME   Elizabeth Block
GHOSTS!   Martine Bellen
GIRAFFES IN HIDING   Carol Novack
GNOSTIC FREQUENCIES   Patrick Pritchett
GOD'S WHISPER   Dennis Barone
GOWANUS CANAL, HANS KNUDSEN   Tod Thilleman
HALF-GIRL   Stephanie Dickinson
HIDDEN DEATH, HIDDEN ESCAPE   Liviu Georgescu

Houndstooth   David Wirthlin
Identity   Basil King
In Times of Danger   Paul Oppenheimer
Incretion   Brian Strang
Inferno   Carmen Firan
Infinity Subsections   Mark DuCharme
Insouciance   Thomas Phillips
Inverted Curvatures   Francis Raven
The Ivory Hour   Laynie Browne
Jackpot   Tsipi Keller
The Jazzer & The Loitering Lady   Gordon Osing
Kissing Nests   Werner Lutz, trans. by Marc Vincenz
Knowledge   Michael Heller
Lady V.   D.R. Popa
Last Supper of the Senses   Dean Kostos
A Lesser Day   Andrea Scrima
Let's Talk About Death   M. Maurice Abitbol
Libretto for the Exhausted World   Michael Fisher
Light House   Brian Lucas
Light Years: Multimedia in the East Village, 1960-1966   (ed.) Carol Bergé
Little Book of Days   Nona Caspers
Little Tales of Family & War   Martha King
Long Fall: Essays and Texts   Andrey Gritsman
Lunacies   Ruxandra Cesereanu
Lust Series   Stephanie Dickinson
Lyrical Interference   Norman Finkelstein
Maine Book   Joe Cardarelli (ed.) Anselm Hollo
MannhatteN   Sarah Rosenthal
Mating In Captivity   Nava Renek
Meanwhile   Gordon Osing
Medieval Ohio   Richard Blevins
Memory's Wake   Derek Owens
Mermaid's Purse   Laynie Browne
Miming Mink   j/j hastain

MOBILITY LOUNGE   David Lincoln
MODERN ADVENTURES   Bill Evans
THE MOSCOVIAD   Yuri Andrukhovych
MULTIFESTO: A HENRI D'MESCAN READER   Davis Schneiderman
MY LAST CENTURY   Joanna Sit
THE NEW BEAUTIFUL TENDONS   Jeffery Beam
NIGHTSHIFT / AN AREA OF SHADOWS   Erika Burkart & Ernst Halter
NO PERFECT WORDS   Nava Renek
NO WRONG NOTES   Norman Weinstein
NORTH & SOUTH   Martha King
NOTES OF A NUDE MODEL   Harriet Sohmers Zwerling
THE NUMBER OF MISSING   Adam Berlin
OF ALL THE CORNERS TO FORGET   Gian Lombardo
ONÖNYXA & THERSEYN   T Thilleman
THE OPENING DAY   Richard Blevins
OUR FATHER   M.G. Stephens
OVER THE LIFELINE   Adrian Sangeorzan
PAGAN DAYS   Michael Rumaker
PART OF THE DESIGN   Laura E. Wright
PIECES FOR SMALL ORCHESTRA & OTHER FICTIONS   Norman Lock
A PLACE IN THE SUN   Lewis Warsh
THE POET : PENCIL PORTRAITS   Basil King
POLITICAL ECOSYSTEMS   J.P. Harpignies
POWERS: TRACK 3   Norman Finkelstein
THE PRISON NOTEBOOKS OF ALAN KRIEGER (TERRORIST)   Marc Estrin
THE PROPAGANDA FACTORY   Marc Vincenz
PSYCHONAUTICA   Paul Doru
COLUMNS: TRACK 2   Norman Finkelstein
REMAINS TO BE SEEN   Halvard Johnson
RETELLING   Tsipi Keller
RIVERING   Dean Kostos
ROOT-CELLAR TO RIVERINE   Tod Thilleman
THE ROOTS OF HUMAN SEXUALITY   M. Maurice Abitbol

SAIGON AND OTHER POEMS   Jack Walters
A SARDINE ON VACATION   Robert Castle
SAVOIR FEAR   Charles Borkhuis
SECRET OF WHITE   Barbara Tomash
SEDUCTION   Lynda Schor
SEE WHAT YOU THINK   David Rosenberg
SETTLEMENT   Martin Nakell
SEX AND THE SENIOR CITY   M. Maurice Abitbol
SKETCHES IN NORSE & FORRA   t thilleman
SKETCHES TZITZIMIME   t thilleman
SLAUGHTERING THE BUDDHA   Gordon Osing
THE SNAIL'S SONG   Alta Ifland
SOS: SONG OF SONGS OF SOLOMON   j/j hastain
THE SPARK SINGER   Jade Sylvan
SPIRITLAND   Nava Renek
STRANGE EVOLUTIONARY FLOWERS   Lizbeth Rymland
SUDDENLY TODAY WE CAN DREAM   Rutha Rosen
THE SUDDEN DEATH OF...   Serge Gavronsky
THE TAKEAWAY BIN   Toni Mirosevich
THE TATTERED LION   Juana Culhane
TAUTOLOGICAL EYE   Martin Nakell
TED'S FAVORITE SKIRT   Lewis Warsh
THEATER OF SKIN   Gordon Osing & Tom Carlson
THINGS THAT NEVER HAPPENED   Gordon Osing
THREAD   Vasyl Makhno
THREE MOUTHS   Tod Thilleman
THREE SEA MONSTERS   Tod Thilleman
TRACK   Norman Finkelstein
TRANSITORY   Jane Augustine
TRANSPARENCIES LIFTED FROM NOON   Chris Glomski
TRIPLE CROWN SONNETS   Jeffrey Cyphers Wright
TSIM-TSUM   Marc Estrin
TWELVE CIRCLES   Yuri Andrukhovych

VIENNA ØØ   Eugene K. Garber
UNCENSORED SONGS FOR SAM ABRAMS   (ed.) John Roche
UP FISH CREEK ROAD   David Matlin
WARP SPASM   Basil King
WATCHFULNESS   Peter O'Leary
WATCH THE DOORS AS THEY CLOSE   Karen Lillis
WALKING AFTER MIDNIGHT   Bill Kushner
WEST OF WEST END   Peter Freund
WHEN THE GODS COME HOME TO ROOST   Marc Estrin
WHIRLIGIG   Christopher Salerno
WHITE, CHRISTIAN   Christopher Stoddard
WINTER LETTERS   Vasyl Makhno
WITHIN THE SPACE BETWEEN   Stacy Cartledge
A WORLD OF NOTHING BUT NATIONS   Tod Thilleman
A WORLD OF NOTHING BUT SELF-INFLICTION   Tod Thilleman
WRECKAGE OF REASON   (ed.) Nava Renek
XIAN DYAD   Jason Price Everett
The YELLOW HOUSE   Robin Behn
YOU, ME, AND THE INSECTS   Barbara Henning

www.ingramcontent.com/pod-product-compliance
Lightning Source LLC
Chambersburg PA
CBHW020919090426
42736CB00008B/700